Resilience Unleashed: The Persian Wars' Impact

Christoffer Smestad

Published by Christoffer Smestad, 2023.

While every precaution has been taken in the preparation of this book, the publisher assumes no responsibility for errors or omissions, or for damages resulting from the use of the information contained herein.

RESILIENCE UNLEASHED: THE PERSIAN WARS' IMPACT

Table of Contents

Chapter 1: The Ionian Revolt 1

Chapter 2: Battle of Marathon... 3

Chapter 3: Xerxes' Preparation 6

Chapter 4: Battle of Thermopylae 9

Chapter 5: Naval Battles of Artemisium and Salamis 12

Chapter 6: Destruction of Athens... 15

Chapter 7: Battle of Plataea 17

Chapter 8: Siege of Athens 20

Chapter 9: The Delian League 23

Chapter 10: The Peace of Callias.. 26

Chapter 11: The Rise of Athens.. 29

Chapter 12: The Thirty Years' Peace 32

Chapter 13: The First Peloponnesian War 35

Chapter 14: The Sicilian Expedition 38

Chapter 15: Spartan Victory 41

Chapter 16: The Peace of Antalcidas.. 44

Chapter 17: Legacy of the Persian Wars 47

Chapter 18: Alexander the Great 50

Chapter 19: Hellenistic Period 53

Chapter 20: Western Civilization 56

Chapter 1: The Ionian Revolt

I n the year 499 BCE, the city-states of Ionia, located on the western coast of present-day Turkey, rose up in rebellion against Persian rule. These Greek settlements had been under Persian control for several decades, but now they sought to regain their independence.

Driven by a desire for self-rule and inspired by the democratic ideals emerging in Athens, the Ionians began their revolt against the Persian Empire. They saw an opportunity to break free from the authority of the Great King and establish their own autonomous city-states.

Athens, a prominent Greek city-state known for its burgeoning democracy and naval power, eagerly supported the Ionian Revolt. Athens saw an opportunity to weaken Persia's grip on the region and expand its own influence. The Athenians sent troops, supplies, and financial aid to aid the Ionian rebels in their struggle for liberation.

Under the leadership of Aristagoras, the tyrant of Miletus, the Ionian cities fought against Persian forces, engaging in battles and skirmishes across the region. However, despite some early successes, the Ionians ultimately faced difficulties. The Persian Empire, with its vast resources and military might, posed a formidable challenge.

Despite their best efforts, the Ionians could not sustain their rebellion indefinitely. The Persian Empire, led by King Darius I, launched a counteroffensive to suppress the revolt and bring the rebellious cities back under Persian control. The Ionian forces, lacking the necessary resources and unified command, struggled to withstand the Persian onslaught.

Eventually, the Ionian Revolt was quashed by the Persian Empire. The cities of Ionia fell one by one to Persian forces, and their hopes for independence were shattered. The Persians brutally punished the rebel cities, making examples of those who dared to challenge their authority.

Although the Ionian Revolt ended in failure, its significance should not be underestimated. The revolt marked a pivotal moment in the escalating tensions between the Greeks and Persians. It set the stage for the larger conflict that would come to be known as the Greco-Persian Wars, as Athens and other Greek city-states would continue their resistance against Persian domination.

The Ionian Revolt also demonstrated the power of Athens and its willingness to support other Greek city-states in their fight against Persian oppression. This early display of solidarity would shape Athens' role in the subsequent Persian Wars, as it emerged as a leader in the defense of Greek freedom and democracy against the Persian Empire.

Chapter 2: Battle of Marathon

In the year 490 BCE, the Persian Empire, under the leadership of King Darius I, launched a full-scale invasion of Greece. Seeking to punish Athens for its involvement in the Ionian Revolt and to extend Persian control over the Greek city-states, the Persian army set its sights on the Athenian homeland.

As news of the Persian invasion reached Athens, the city-state called upon its allies for aid. A coalition of Greek city-states, led by Athens and its renowned general Miltiades, assembled to defend their lands against the Persian forces.

The Persian army, numbering in the tens of thousands, landed on the plain of Marathon, northeast of Athens. Aware of the overwhelming Persian numbers, Miltiades devised a bold strategy. Rather than waiting to be attacked, he decided to take the initiative and launch a preemptive strike against the Persians.

Miltiades deployed his forces on the plain of Marathon, positioning his hoplite infantry in the center and reinforcing the flanks. The Athenian army, though significantly outnumbered, displayed exceptional discipline and cohesion.

When the battle commenced, the Persians launched their attack, hoping to break through the Greek lines and claim victory. However, the disciplined Greek hoplites held their ground and repelled wave after wave of Persian assaults.

Miltiades, recognizing a weakness in the Persian formation, ordered a strategic maneuver known as the "double envelopment." The Greek wings pushed forward, encircling the Persian center and effectively cutting off their retreat.

Caught off guard by the Greek maneuver and facing heavy casualties, the Persian army began to falter. Meanwhile, the Greek hoplites fought with remarkable determination and skill, driving the Persians back and inflicting significant losses.

In the end, the Battle of Marathon proved to be a stunning victory for the Greeks. Despite being vastly outnumbered, the Athenians and their allies succeeded in repelling the Persian invasion force.

Thousands of Persian soldiers were killed, while the Greek casualties were relatively minimal. The Athenians, who played a crucial role in the battle, emerged as heroes, boosting their confidence and pride. It was a resounding triumph that bolstered Greek morale and sent shockwaves throughout the Persian Empire.

Following their victory, the Athenians dispatched a messenger named Pheidippides to bring news of the triumph back to Athens. According to legend, Pheidippides ran the entire distance from Marathon to Athens, a distance of about 26 miles, without stopping, to deliver the momentous news. This feat would later inspire the creation of the modern-day marathon race.

The Battle of Marathon became a defining moment in Greek history and a symbol of courage and determination. It showcased the potential of Greek city-states to resist Persian aggression and inspired a sense of unity and resilience among the Greeks as they prepared for future conflicts against the Persian Empire.

Chapter 3: Xerxes' Preparation

Years after the Battle of Marathon, in 480 BCE, King Xerxes I ascended the Persian throne following the death of his father, Darius I. Determined to avenge the Persian defeat at Marathon and to extend Persian dominion over Greece, Xerxes embarked on an ambitious campaign to conquer the Greek city-states.

Xerxes immediately set about preparing for the invasion, recognizing the need for a formidable military force and a powerful navy to achieve his objectives. He sought to surpass the previous Persian expedition in scale and effectiveness.

One of Xerxes' notable achievements was the construction of a massive pontoon bridge across the Hellespont (now known as the Dardanelles). This bridge allowed his army to cross the narrow strait from Asia into Europe, facilitating the movement of troops and supplies. The construction of the bridge demonstrated the vast resources and organizational capabilities of the Persian Empire.

To assemble his forces, Xerxes called upon the diverse nations within his empire. Persians, Medes, Assyrians, Babylonians, Egyptians, and numerous other subject peoples contributed soldiers, forming a colossal army. Estimates of the size of Xerxes' army vary, but it is believed to have numbered in the hundreds of thousands, possibly even exceeding one million men.

Alongside the land forces, Xerxes amassed a formidable naval fleet. Recognizing the significance of naval power in the Greek theater of war, he assembled a vast armada of warships and supply vessels. The Persian fleet included triremes, advanced warships equipped with three banks of oars and formidable naval weaponry.

With his forces assembled, Xerxes embarked on his grand expedition. The Persian army, accompanied by the naval fleet, moved from Asia Minor towards Greece, advancing through Thrace and Macedonia.

As the Persians progressed, they encountered little resistance from the Greek city-states, many of which had been divided in their approach to the impending invasion. Some city-states, such as Thebes and Thessaly, submitted to Persian authority, while others, like Athens and Sparta, remained defiant.

Xerxes' preparations extended beyond military might. He also sought to demonstrate his grandeur and power through lavish displays and infrastructure projects. Xerxes commissioned the construction of the Gate of All Nations and the massive palace complex at Persepolis, showcasing Persian architectural prowess.

As Xerxes' invasion force approached Greece, the stage was set for a climactic clash between Persian might and Greek determination. The Greek city-states, despite their internal divisions, began to unite in the face of the looming Persian threat, rallying behind the leadership of Athens and Sparta.

The stage was now set for the decisive battles of the Greco-Persian Wars, as Xerxes and his vast army and fleet prepared to confront the Greeks on their own soil. The outcome of this epic struggle would shape the course of history and determine the fate of Greece and its enduring legacy.

Chapter 4: Battle of Thermopylae

In 480 BCE, as King Xerxes I of Persia led his massive army through Greece, one small Greek force stood in his path. At the pass of Thermopylae, King Leonidas I of Sparta, with a contingent of around 300 Spartans and several thousand Greek allies, made a valiant stand against the Persian invasion.

Thermopylae, a narrow mountain pass in central Greece, offered a strategic advantage for the Greek defenders. The rugged terrain and limited space negated the numerical advantage of the Persian forces, making it an ideal location for a small force to hold off a much larger army.

Leonidas, renowned for Spartan discipline and bravery, led his warriors with unwavering determination. They formed a defensive phalanx, a tightly packed formation of overlapping shields and spears, ready to withstand the Persian onslaught.

For three days, the Greeks held their ground, repelling wave after wave of Persian attacks. The Spartans, renowned for their military prowess, fought with unmatched ferocity, pushing back the Persian forces and inflicting heavy casualties.

However, a local resident named Ephialtes betrayed the Greeks by revealing a mountain path that led behind the Greek lines. Learning of this treachery, Leonidas realized the imminent danger to his flanks and made the difficult decision to dismiss most of the Greek allies, remaining with his 300 Spartans and a small contingent of Thespians.

On the final day of the battle, the Persians, now aware of the mountain path, launched a two-pronged attack, surrounding the Greek defenders. Despite their fierce resistance, the Greeks found themselves overwhelmed by the sheer number of Persian troops.

Leonidas, knowing the battle was lost, ordered his Spartans to fall back while he and a few loyal warriors, including the Thespians, stayed behind to cover their retreat. In a last stand of immense bravery, they fought to the death, refusing to surrender.

The Battle of Thermopylae ended in a Persian victory, with the Greek defenders ultimately succumbing to the overwhelming forces arrayed against them. However, the heroic sacrifice of Leonidas and his warriors left an indelible mark on history.

Their bravery and unwavering dedication to their homeland elevated the Battle of Thermopylae into legend. The sacrifice of the Spartans became a symbol of the extraordinary courage and resilience of the Greek city-states in the face of Persian aggression.

Leonidas and his warriors gained legendary status, celebrated for their bravery and selflessness. Their sacrifice at Thermopylae became a rallying cry for the Greeks, fueling their determination to continue the fight against the Persians and defend their freedom.

The Battle of Thermopylae, although a tactical defeat for the Greeks, served as a powerful inspiration for subsequent battles in the Persian Wars. It demonstrated that even against overwhelming odds, a small force could stand against tyranny and leave an enduring legacy of heroism.

Chapter 5: Naval Battles of Artemisium and Salamis

———

As the Persian forces pushed through the pass of Thermopylae and made their way further into Greece, the Greek naval forces prepared to meet the Persian fleet in a series of crucial naval battles.

The first engagement took place at the straits of Artemisium, near the island of Euboea. The Greek fleet, consisting of ships from various city-states, faced the formidable Persian armada, led by the experienced Persian admiral, Artemisia.

At Artemisium, the Greeks initially faced setbacks as they encountered the sheer size and strength of the Persian fleet. However, through their superior seamanship and tactical skill, the Greeks managed to hold their ground, inflicting heavy losses upon the Persian navy.

Despite the valiant efforts of both sides, the naval battle at Artemisium ended inconclusively. Yet, it provided the Greeks with a glimmer of hope, showing that they could resist the Persian naval power.

Meanwhile, back on land, the Greeks faced a devastating defeat at the Battle of Thermopylae, resulting in the fall of Leonidas and his brave Spartans. The news of this setback sent shockwaves throughout the Greek city-states, but it also heightened their resolve to continue the fight against the Persian invaders.

With their morale bolstered by their performance at Artemisium, the Greek naval forces, now under the leadership of the Athenian general Themistocles, prepared for the next decisive confrontation with the Persians.

The stage was set for the Battle of Salamis, a naval engagement that would prove to be a turning point in the Persian Wars. The Persian fleet, led by King Xerxes himself, outnumbered the Greek ships by a significant margin. The Persians were confident that their overwhelming numerical advantage would ensure victory.

Themistocles, aware of the Greeks' disadvantage in numbers, devised a clever strategy. He convinced the Greek commanders to lure the Persian fleet into the narrow straits of Salamis, where the larger Persian ships would be hindered by the confined space, negating their numerical superiority.

As the Persian fleet entered the straits, the Greek ships launched a coordinated attack. With exceptional skill and precision, the Greek sailors maneuvered their smaller, more agile triremes, ramming into Persian vessels and causing chaos within the enemy ranks.

The Greeks exploited their knowledge of the local waters and used the narrow channels to their advantage, effectively trapping and destroying numerous Persian ships. The Persian navy, unable to maneuver effectively, suffered heavy losses as their ships collided with one another and were left vulnerable to Greek attacks.

The Battle of Salamis ended in a resounding Greek victory. The Persian fleet, severely weakened and demoralized, retreated, leaving behind a significant portion of their ships in the waters surrounding Salamis.

The Greek triumph at Salamis was a crucial turning point in the Persian Wars. The decisive victory not only thwarted the Persian naval dominance but also boosted Greek morale and unified the city-states in their resistance against the Persian invaders.

The combined efforts of the Greek naval forces at Artemisium and Salamis demonstrated the effectiveness of their naval tactics and highlighted their determination to defend their freedom and way of life.

The naval victories of Artemisium and Salamis significantly weakened the Persian forces and paved the way for subsequent Greek successes in repelling the Persian invasion. The Greeks had proven that, even against overwhelming odds, their courage, skill, and unity could overcome the might of the Persian Empire.

Chapter 6: Destruction of Athens

As the Persian forces continued their advance into Greece, the city of Athens faced an imminent threat. Recognizing the danger, the Athenians made the difficult decision to evacuate their beloved city and seek refuge elsewhere.

The citizens of Athens hastily gathered their belongings and made their way to the port, where a fleet of ships awaited them. Families, soldiers, and scholars alike boarded the vessels, leaving behind their homes and temples, knowing that their city was about to fall into the hands of the Persians.

With heavy hearts, the Athenians departed, their hopes and dreams intertwined with the fate of their city. The Persians, led by King Xerxes, soon arrived in Athens, finding the city empty of its inhabitants.

In an act of retribution and to showcase their power, the Persian forces ransacked and burned Athens. Temples, monuments, and homes that once stood as testaments to the glory of the city were reduced to ashes. The Persian soldiers looted precious treasures and desecrated sacred sites, leaving a trail of destruction in their wake.

Yet, despite the devastation, the spirit of the Athenians remained unbroken. Rather than dwelling on the loss of their city, they turned their attention to their naval strength and the hope that lay within their fleet.

The Athenians, known for their naval prowess and maritime tradition, realized that their strength lay in their ability to control the sea. They regrouped and made their way to the nearby island of Salamis, which offered a strategic location for their naval operations.

On Salamis, the Athenians found solace and reestablished their unity. They concentrated their efforts on building and reinforcing their fleet, knowing that it would be their key to resisting the Persian invasion and reclaiming their homeland.

The destruction of Athens, while a devastating blow, served to strengthen the resolve of the Athenians. The sight of their city in ruins fueled their determination to fight back and ensure that the sacrifices made by their fellow citizens would not be in vain.

As the Greeks gathered on the island of Salamis, they prepared for the upcoming battles that would determine the fate of their land. They knew that their naval strength, combined with their unwavering spirit, would play a crucial role in the ongoing struggle against the Persians.

The Athenians, united with their fellow Greek city-states, set their sights on the next stage of the conflict, eager to confront the Persian forces once again and reclaim their homeland from the clutches of destruction.

Chapter 7: Battle of Plataea

In the year 479 BCE, the Greek city-states, recognizing the imminent threat posed by the Persians, set aside their differences and forged a united front. Determined to defend their freedom and way of life, they assembled a combined force to confront the Persian invaders once and for all.

The Battle of Plataea would prove to be a pivotal moment in the Persian Wars. It would determine whether Greece would fall under the dominance of the Persian Empire or emerge victorious, securing its independence.

Led by their respective leaders, the Greek city-states marched to the plains of Plataea, where they awaited the approaching Persian army. The combined Greek force consisted of warriors from Sparta, Athens, Corinth, Thebes, and numerous other city-states. Their unity symbolized a shared determination to repel the Persian aggression.

The Persian army, commanded by Mardonius, consisted of a formidable force, fueled by the desire to avenge the earlier defeats and establish Persian dominance over Greece once and for all. They believed their vast numbers and military might would secure their victory.

The battle commenced with fierce clashes between the opposing forces. The Greek hoplites, heavily armored and disciplined, formed an unyielding phalanx, their shields interlocked, and spears extended. They withstood the Persian assaults, standing their ground and inflicting heavy casualties upon their foes.

The Greeks, fortified by their sense of unity and the knowledge that the fate of their homeland hung in the balance, fought with unmatched determination. The Spartans, renowned for their warrior ethos, led the charge, their presence instilling fear in the hearts of their enemies.

The battle raged on for hours, with both sides locked in a brutal struggle for supremacy. However, it was the Greek tactics and superior discipline that would ultimately tip the scales in their favor.

Recognizing the importance of maintaining a solid defensive line, the Greeks gradually gained the upper hand, systematically pushing back the Persian forces. The Persians, facing a united and determined enemy, struggled to maintain their cohesion as the Greeks relentlessly pressed forward.

In a decisive turn of events, Mardonius, the Persian commander, fell in battle, further demoralizing his troops. Sensing victory within their grasp, the Greeks redoubled their efforts, rallying together to deliver a final blow.

The Persian army, now disoriented and in disarray, retreated in a state of defeat. The Battle of Plataea marked a resounding triumph for the Greeks, dealing a significant blow to Persian ambitions of conquest.

The victory at Plataea not only halted the Persian advance but also bolstered the morale of the Greek city-states. It showcased the power of their unity and collective resolve in the face of adversity. The Greeks had proven that their city-states, when united, could stand against the mightiest empire of the time.

The Battle of Plataea served as a turning point in the Persian Wars. It shattered the Persian dream of subjugating Greece and preserving the freedom and independence of the Greek city-states. The Greeks celebrated their victory, recognizing the sacrifices made by their warriors and the significance of their united front.

With the Battle of Plataea behind them, the Greeks now turned their attention to further pushing back the Persian forces and reclaiming their lands. Their triumph at Plataea emboldened them, fueling their determination to defend their homeland and ensure a future free from Persian domination.

Chapter 8: Siege of Athens

Following the decisive victory at the Battle of Plataea, the Greek city-states, filled with renewed vigor and determination, turned their attention towards liberating Athens from Persian control. With their combined forces, they marched back to their beloved city, ready to reclaim it from the clutches of the invaders.

As the Greek army approached Athens, the Persian garrison stationed there realized that their time was running out. They could no longer hold the city against the overwhelming force of the victorious Greeks. The Persians prepared for a last stand, knowing that defeat was imminent.

The siege of Athens began, as the Greek forces encircled the city, cutting off supply lines and preventing any potential reinforcements or escape for the remaining Persian soldiers. The Greeks were resolute in their mission to liberate their city and restore its former glory.

The siege lasted for several weeks, with both sides engaged in intense skirmishes and sporadic clashes. The Greeks utilized their superior military tactics, implementing siege engines and gradually weakening the defenses of the Persian garrison.

As the days turned into weeks, the Persian soldiers, realizing the futility of their resistance, faced a difficult decision. Surrendering to the Greeks would mean the end of their control over Athens, but they would likely be spared from further harm. On the other hand, if they chose to fight to the bitter end, they risked annihilation.

In a final act of defiance, the Persian garrison launched a desperate counterattack. The battle within the city's walls was fierce, with Greek and Persian warriors locked in deadly combat. However, the overwhelming numbers and determination of the Greek forces proved insurmountable.

The Greeks gradually gained the upper hand, pushing deeper into the city and forcing the remaining Persian soldiers into a small, fortified area. Realizing the inevitable, the Persian commander chose to surrender, recognizing that further resistance would only lead to unnecessary bloodshed.

With the Persian garrison defeated and Athens liberated, the Greek soldiers and the returning Athenian citizens rejoiced. The city, though ravaged by war and fire, held the promise of a brighter future. The long process of reconstruction and recovery began.

The Athenians, filled with a sense of pride and determination, embarked on the arduous task of rebuilding their beloved city. The reconstruction efforts were vast, as the Athenians aimed to restore their iconic temples, public buildings, and homes to their former grandeur.

The victory in the siege of Athens symbolized not only the expulsion of the Persian invaders but also the resilience and indomitable spirit of the Athenians. They were determined to rise from the ashes and rebuild their city, ensuring that Athens would once again be a beacon of culture, philosophy, and democracy.

The recovery of Athens was a collective effort, as citizens, artisans, and builders worked tirelessly to reconstruct what had been lost. It was a testament to the Athenians' unwavering commitment to their city and their determination to preserve their way of life.

Over time, Athens emerged from the devastation of war, gradually regaining its former glory. The reconstruction efforts breathed new life into the city, and its inhabitants worked towards creating a society that embodied the values of democracy, learning, and artistic expression.

The siege of Athens marked a significant milestone in the Persian Wars, as the city's liberation not only symbolized the triumph of the Greek city-states but also served as a testament to their collective strength and resilience. Athens stood as a symbol of Greek unity and the enduring spirit that could not be extinguished by the forces of invasion.

As the city began to thrive once again, the Athenians looked towards the future, understanding the importance of safeguarding their newfound freedom and ensuring that the lessons learned from the Persian Wars would shape their society for generations to come.

Chapter 9: The Delian League

In the aftermath of the Persian Wars and the successful liberation of Athens, the Athenians recognized the need for a unified defense against future Persian invasions. To safeguard the independence and security of the Greek city-states, Athens took the initiative to form an alliance known as the Delian League.

The Delian League was established as a collective defense pact, with participating city-states pledging their military support and resources to prevent any potential Persian incursions. Under the leadership of Athens, the league aimed to create a strong and unified force that would deter future Persian aggression and protect the Greek territories.

Initially, the league's headquarters were located on the island of Delos, which served as a symbolic meeting point for the member states. Contributions from the member city-states were pooled together to form a common treasury, which would finance the league's military endeavors and maintain a formidable naval fleet.

As the league grew in strength and influence, Athens emerged as its de facto leader. The Athenians, capitalizing on their naval power and political astuteness, gradually assumed a dominant role within the league, shaping its policies and decisions.

Under Athenian leadership, the Delian League became more than just a defensive alliance. It evolved into a vehicle for

Athenian imperialism, as Athens used its position to extend its influence and exert control over the member states. The league transformed into an instrument of Athenian hegemony, with other city-states becoming increasingly dependent on Athens for protection and guidance.

Athens, renowned for its democratic ideals and cultural achievements, effectively utilized its influence within the league to promote its democratic principles and spread its cultural values. The city-state fostered a sense of unity among the member states through cultural and intellectual exchange, encouraging the development of arts, philosophy, and architecture.

The Delian League, under Athenian leadership, embarked on numerous military campaigns to safeguard its interests and protect its member states. Athenian naval dominance was instrumental in repelling potential Persian threats and maintaining the league's supremacy in the Aegean region.

However, as Athens consolidated its power within the league, tensions arose among the member states. Some city-states began to resent the increasing control and dominance exerted by Athens. What was initially conceived as a defensive alliance gradually transformed into a tool for Athenian imperialism, leading to dissent and challenges to Athenian authority.

Nevertheless, the Delian League, despite its flaws and internal divisions, remained a significant force in shaping the geopolitical landscape of ancient Greece. Under Athenian leadership, it played a crucial role in maintaining stability and deterring further Persian invasions.

The legacy of the Delian League extends beyond its military and political achievements. It served as a platform for cultural exchange, intellectual pursuits, and the spread of democratic ideals throughout the Greek city-states. Athens, as the leader of the league, left an indelible mark on the development of Western civilization, with its contributions to philosophy, drama, and political thought.

The Delian League stands as a testament to the power of unity and collective action. It showcased the ability of the Greek city-states to set aside their differences and work together for a common cause, forging a legacy that would influence the course of history.

Chapter 10: The Peace of Callias

Around the year 449 BCE, a significant event known as the Peace of Callias marked the culmination of the Greco-Persian Wars and brought a sense of stability to the region. Named after the Athenian statesman Callias, who played a prominent role in its negotiation, the peace treaty represented a crucial diplomatic achievement between Persia and Greece.

The Peace of Callias signified a significant shift in the dynamics between the Persian Empire and the Greek city-states. Through this treaty, Persia recognized the autonomy of the Greek city-states in Asia Minor, granting them the freedom to govern themselves without Persian interference.

The negotiations leading to the Peace of Callias were complex, involving diplomats and representatives from both sides. The treaty aimed to establish a lasting peace, ending decades of conflict and providing a framework for peaceful coexistence in the region.

Under the terms of the peace treaty, Persia formally acknowledged the territorial integrity and political independence of the Greek city-states in Asia Minor. This recognition was a significant victory for the Greeks, as it granted them the freedom to govern themselves without Persian interference or control.

The signing of the Peace of Callias brought a sense of relief and stability to the region. It represented a turning point in the Greco-Persian Wars, signifying the end of open hostilities and the beginning of a new era characterized by peaceful relations and respect for each other's sovereignty.

With the peace treaty in place, the Greek city-states in Asia Minor could focus on rebuilding their communities and developing their societies without the constant threat of Persian invasions. The autonomy granted to them provided a sense of security and a foundation for the flourishing of their cultural and political institutions.

The Peace of Callias also had broader implications for the geopolitical balance in the ancient world. It marked a shift in the power dynamics between the Persian Empire and the Greek city-states, with Persia recognizing the resilience and strength of the Greeks. The treaty demonstrated that the Greeks, through their unity and determination, could successfully resist Persian aggression and secure their freedom.

The peace achieved through the treaty was not just a cessation of hostilities but also a recognition of the importance of diplomacy and negotiation in resolving conflicts. It set a precedent for future diplomatic efforts and highlighted the potential for peaceful resolutions to disputes.

While the Peace of Callias brought a temporary respite to the conflicts between Persia and Greece, it did not completely eliminate tensions or rivalries in the region. The legacy of the

Greco-Persian Wars would continue to shape the relationships between these powers and influence the course of history.

Nonetheless, the Peace of Callias remains a significant milestone in ancient Greek history. It represents a moment of triumph for the Greek city-states, as they secured their autonomy and established the foundation for future diplomatic engagements. The peace treaty stands as a testament to the power of negotiation and the desire for a peaceful coexistence in a region marked by decades of conflict.

Chapter 11: The Rise of Athens

With the establishment of the Delian League and the consolidation of its power, Athens emerged as a prominent force in ancient Greece. The city-state used the league as a platform to extend its influence and lay the foundation for what would become the Athenian Empire. Under the leadership of statesmen like Pericles, Athens experienced a golden age of democracy, culture, and intellectual achievement.

As Athens grew in strength and confidence, it sought to assert its dominance over other city-states within the league. It gradually transformed the alliance into an empire, with Athens at its helm. The league's treasury, initially established for collective defense, became a source of wealth for Athens, allowing the city-state to finance ambitious projects and expand its sphere of influence.

Pericles, a charismatic and influential leader, rose to prominence during this period. He became the dominant figure in Athenian politics and played a pivotal role in shaping the city-state's destiny. Pericles advocated for democratic principles and implemented policies that enhanced the power and prestige of Athens.

Under Pericles' leadership, Athens experienced a cultural and intellectual renaissance. The city-state became a hub of artistic expression, philosophical inquiry, and architectural innovation. The Parthenon, a symbol of Athenian democracy and a testament to its architectural prowess, was constructed during this period.

The Athenian democracy flourished, with an emphasis on citizen participation, public debate, and the rule of law. The city-state became a beacon of democracy, attracting thinkers, artists, and philosophers from across the Greek world. Figures like Socrates, Plato, and Aristotle emerged during this time, contributing to the development of Western philosophy and thought.

The Athenian Empire, established through the influence and resources of the Delian League, extended its reach beyond the city-state itself. Athens formed alliances, imposed its own political systems on conquered territories, and demanded tribute from the subject states. The empire's maritime strength, bolstered by a formidable navy, allowed Athens to control trade routes, enforce its policies, and project its power throughout the Aegean and beyond.

However, the rise of Athens and the Athenian Empire did not come without controversy and opposition. Other city-states within the league grew resentful of Athens' dominance and began to question its motivations. The Peloponnesian League, led by Sparta, emerged as a rival power, challenging Athens' supremacy and ultimately leading to the devastating Peloponnesian War.

Despite the eventual decline and fall of the Athenian Empire, the period of its rise marked a remarkable chapter in history. Athens, under the visionary leadership of Pericles, experienced a cultural and intellectual flourishing that would leave an indelible impact on Western civilization.

The rise of Athens showcased the transformative power of democracy, cultural patronage, and intellectual pursuits. It demonstrated the potential of a city-state to rise above its rivals and become a center of influence, innovation, and inspiration.

The legacy of Athens' golden age continues to resonate in the fields of politics, philosophy, art, and architecture. Its democratic ideals and cultural achievements have shaped the foundations of modern Western societies and serve as a reminder of the heights that human civilization can reach when guided by vision, creativity, and the pursuit of knowledge.

Chapter 12: The Thirty Years' Peace

In 446 BCE, a significant event known as the Thirty Years' Peace brought an end to the ongoing conflicts between Athens and Sparta, two of the most powerful Greek city-states. This peace treaty, negotiated between the two rivals, aimed to establish a period of stability and prevent further bloodshed.

The Thirty Years' Peace was a product of the desire for a lasting resolution and the recognition of the toll that continuous warfare had taken on both Athens and Sparta. The terms of the peace agreement outlined a thirty-year period of non-aggression and established a framework for resolving disputes through diplomatic means rather than armed conflict.

Under the terms of the treaty, both Athens and Sparta agreed to respect each other's territorial integrity and autonomy. The city-states committed to refraining from military actions and to settling disputes through negotiation and arbitration.

On the surface, the Thirty Years' Peace brought a sense of relief to the Greek world. It provided a respite from the conflicts that had plagued the region for decades, allowing the city-states to focus on rebuilding their societies and strengthening their economies. Trade and cultural exchange flourished during this period, contributing to a sense of stability and prosperity.

However, tensions between Athens and Sparta continued to simmer beneath the surface, despite the peace agreement. The two city-states remained wary of each other's ambitions and sought to assert their influence in different ways. Athens continued to expand its empire through its control over the Delian League, while Sparta sought to consolidate its power within the Peloponnesian League.

The unresolved issues and lingering resentments would eventually lead to the outbreak of the Peloponnesian War in 431 BCE, shattering the fragile peace established by the Thirty Years' Peace. The underlying tensions and rivalries between Athens and Sparta proved too great to be contained, and the subsequent war would engulf the Greek city-states, bringing widespread devastation and fundamentally altering the balance of power in the region.

While the Thirty Years' Peace failed to provide a long-lasting resolution to the conflicts between Athens and Sparta, it did serve as a temporary period of stability and allowed for some economic and cultural growth. The peace agreement demonstrated the recognition among the city-states of the need for a more diplomatic approach to resolving disputes, even if it ultimately proved insufficient in preventing the eruption of future conflicts.

The legacy of the Thirty Years' Peace lies in its reminder of the complexities and challenges of maintaining peace in a region marked by intense rivalries and power struggles. It serves as a cautionary tale of the fragility of agreements and the need for sustained efforts to address underlying grievances and foster genuine reconciliation.

The Thirty Years' Peace represents a significant chapter in ancient Greek history, highlighting the aspirations for peace and stability amidst the complexities of interstate relations. Its eventual failure underscores the difficulties of achieving lasting harmony in a world driven by competing interests and ambitions.

Chapter 13: The First Peloponnesian War

In 431 BCE, tensions that had been simmering between Athens and Sparta erupted into a full-scale conflict known as the Peloponnesian War. This war, which lasted for several years, would profoundly impact the Greek city-states and reshape the balance of power in the region.

The causes of the war were multifaceted and intertwined with the underlying rivalries and grievances between Athens and Sparta. Athens, with its growing empire and dominance over the Delian League, had become a source of concern for Sparta and its allies in the Peloponnesian League. Sparta saw Athens as a threat to its own position as the leading city-state in Greece and sought to curtail its power.

The war unfolded through a series of military campaigns, shifting alliances, and battles on both land and sea. Athens, with its formidable navy, initially held the advantage in naval engagements, while Sparta, renowned for its disciplined hoplite soldiers, was stronger on land.

The conflict saw both sides employing different strategies. Athens, under the guidance of Pericles, adopted a defensive approach, utilizing its naval supremacy to protect its empire and maintain control over the sea. Meanwhile, Sparta aimed to weaken Athens by ravaging its territories and challenging its dominance.

The war witnessed notable events and battles, such as the Siege of Potidaea, the Battle of Sybota, and the Battle of Pylos. Athens suffered a devastating blow in 429 BCE when a deadly plague struck the city, causing significant loss of life, including the death of Pericles. This further weakened Athens but did not diminish its resolve to continue the fight.

As the war dragged on, it became increasingly clear that neither side could secure a decisive victory. The conflict brought immense suffering to the Greek city-states, with widespread destruction, economic hardship, and loss of life. It also strained the alliances between various city-states, as they faced difficult decisions regarding their loyalties.

In 421 BCE, both Athens and Sparta agreed to a temporary truce known as the Peace of Nicias, named after the Athenian general Nicias. This peace treaty aimed to halt hostilities and provide a period of respite for both sides. However, it proved to be short-lived, as the underlying tensions and grievances resurfaced.

The Peloponnesian War would continue for several more years, marked by further military campaigns, sieges, and naval battles. Eventually, in 404 BCE, Athens surrendered to Sparta, bringing an end to the first phase of the Peloponnesian War.

The war's consequences were far-reaching. Athens' power and influence were significantly diminished, while Sparta emerged as the dominant force in Greece. The war highlighted the destructive nature of internal conflicts and the fragility of alliances among the Greek city-states.

The Peloponnesian War also had broader implications beyond Greece. It weakened the Greek city-states as a whole, making them vulnerable to outside invasions and interventions. It paved the way for the rise of Macedonia under Philip II and his son, Alexander the Great, who would go on to conquer much of the known world.

The first Peloponnesian War serves as a cautionary tale of the perils of internal strife and the devastating consequences of unchecked rivalries among states. It underscores the complexities of interstate relations and the challenges of achieving lasting peace in a region marked by competing interests and aspirations.

The war would leave an indelible mark on Greek history, influencing the subsequent developments in the ancient world and serving as a reminder of the cost of discord and the pursuit of power at the expense of unity and cooperation.

Chapter 14: The Sicilian Expedition

In 415 BCE, during the Peloponnesian War, Athens embarked on a grand and ambitious campaign known as the Sicilian Expedition. This military venture aimed to expand Athens' influence by attacking the city of Syracuse in Sicily, a powerful state and a rival to Athens.

The Sicilian Expedition was driven by various factors. Athens sought to gain additional resources, wealth, and strategic advantages by capturing Syracuse. The city was known for its prosperous economy and strong military, and its defeat would have significantly weakened Sparta's allies in the region.

The Athenians assembled a formidable force for the expedition, including a large fleet, numerous soldiers, and supplies. They hoped to exploit the internal divisions within Syracuse and its allies to secure an easy victory and establish a foothold in Sicily.

Initially, the Athenians achieved some success, winning early battles and gaining support from certain Sicilian city-states. However, their advantage quickly turned into a series of setbacks and misfortunes. The Athenian general Nicias, who had advocated for caution and had doubts about the expedition's viability, found his concerns validated.

Syracuse, under the leadership of the general Hermocrates, proved to be a resilient opponent. They rallied their forces, strengthened their defenses, and received reinforcements from other Greek city-states. The Athenians faced fierce resistance and found their initial progress halted.

The Athenian expedition faced numerous challenges, including the unfamiliar terrain of Sicily, difficulties in supply lines, and the determination of Syracuse's defenders. The Athenians also encountered setbacks due to internal disagreements and the lack of effective leadership. These factors, coupled with a series of tactical errors, turned the expedition into a disaster.

The Athenians' situation worsened when a Spartan fleet arrived to support Syracuse, reinforcing the defenders and further tilting the balance against Athens. The Syracuse-Sparta alliance launched a counteroffensive, inflicting heavy losses on the Athenian forces and trapping them within the city's walls.

The siege of Syracuse became a protracted and grueling affair, with the Athenians enduring hunger, disease, and relentless attacks. Their hopes for a swift victory shattered, and their resources depleted, the Athenians faced a desperate struggle for survival.

In 413 BCE, after a long and devastating siege, the Athenians were decisively defeated. Their remaining forces were either killed, captured, or scattered. The Sicilian Expedition ended in a catastrophic failure for Athens, dealing a severe blow to its military strength, resources, and morale.

The defeat in Sicily marked a turning point in the Peloponnesian War. It weakened Athens considerably, eroding its naval supremacy and diminishing its chances of ultimate victory. The loss also emboldened Sparta and its allies, who saw an opportunity to press their advantage and further undermine Athens.

The failed Sicilian Expedition had far-reaching consequences beyond the immediate military setback. It drained Athens' resources and manpower, exacerbating the strains on its empire and weakening its position in the war. The defeat also led to internal turmoil within Athens, with political factions vying for power and scapegoats being sought for the disastrous campaign.

The Sicilian Expedition stands as a cautionary tale of overreach and the dangers of hubris in military endeavors. It highlights the risks of underestimating the strength and resolve of one's opponents, as well as the perils of embarking on grandiose campaigns without adequate planning, intelligence, and resources.

The defeat in Sicily ultimately contributed to Athens' decline and eventual surrender to Sparta in 404 BCE, marking the end of the Peloponnesian War and a significant shift in the balance of power in ancient Greece.

The Sicilian Expedition remains a stark reminder of the fickle nature of war, where the most audacious plans can unravel in the face of determined resistance and unforeseen challenges.

Chapter 15: Spartan Victory

As the Peloponnesian War dragged on, Sparta began to gain the upper hand over Athens. The conflict had taken a toll on both sides, but Sparta managed to secure crucial support from the Persian Empire, which greatly bolstered its resources and military capabilities.

With Persian assistance, Sparta was able to strengthen its navy and expand its military forces. The Persians, seeking to weaken Athens and protect their own interests, provided financial aid and naval support to Sparta. This alliance shifted the balance of power in favor of the Spartan-led Peloponnesian League.

Athens, on the other hand, faced a devastating setback in the form of a deadly plague that struck the city in 430 BCE. This epidemic, known as the Plague of Athens, ravaged the population, claiming the lives of thousands, including the prominent Athenian leader Pericles. The plague not only weakened Athens physically but also dealt a blow to its morale and stability.

The combination of Sparta's strengthened position and Athens' weakened state proved decisive. Sparta and its allies launched a series of successful military campaigns, retaking territories previously under Athenian control. The Spartan general Lysander emerged as a formidable leader, implementing effective strategies that exploited Athens' vulnerabilities.

In 404 BCE, Athens, battered by years of war, internal strife, and deprivation, finally reached a point of surrender. The Spartan forces, led by Lysander, laid siege to Athens, cutting off its vital supply routes and forcing the city into submission. The long and arduous Peloponnesian War had come to an end, with Sparta emerging as the victor.

The terms of Athens' surrender were harsh. The city was forced to dismantle its walls, surrender its fleet, and accept Spartan control. The Athenians also had to renounce their imperial ambitions and submit to the authority of Sparta. The defeat marked the end of Athens' golden age and the loss of its dominant position in Greece.

The Spartan victory and the subsequent dismantling of Athens' power had a significant impact on the Greek world. Sparta, now the dominant city-state, sought to establish its hegemony over the Greek city-states and enforce a more conservative and traditional political order.

However, Sparta's attempts to maintain its control were met with resistance and resentment from other Greek city-states. The fragile balance of power and shifting alliances among the various city-states would lead to further conflicts and struggles for dominance in the years that followed.

The Peloponnesian War and the Spartan victory served as a turning point in Greek history. It marked the end of the democratic experiment in Athens and the rise of Sparta as the leading power. The war's impact extended beyond Greece, as it created a power vacuum that would eventually be filled by the rising kingdom of Macedonia under the leadership of Philip II and his son, Alexander the Great.

The Spartan victory serves as a reminder of the unpredictable nature of warfare and the consequences of prolonged conflicts. It highlights the importance of alliances, resources, and strategic maneuvering in determining the outcome of wars. The fall of Athens, once a powerful and influential city-state, demonstrates the fragility of even the mightiest empires when faced with determined adversaries and internal challenges.

The legacy of the Peloponnesian War and the Spartan victory resonates throughout history, underscoring the complexities of power struggles, the limitations of military might, and the enduring impact of conflict on societies and civilizations.

Chapter 16: The Peace of Antalcidas

In 387 BCE, the Peace of Antalcidas was signed, marking the official end of the Peloponnesian War and ushering in a new era in Greek politics. This peace treaty, also known as the King's Peace, was negotiated by the Spartan general Antalcidas and representatives from various Greek city-states.

The Peace of Antalcidas was unique in that it involved not only Greek city-states but also the Persian Empire, which played a significant role in the negotiations. The Persian king, Artaxerxes II, sought to exert his influence over the Greek world and exploit the weakened state of the city-states after years of war.

Under the terms of the peace treaty, it was agreed that all Greek city-states, both mainland and those located in Asia Minor, would be granted autonomy. However, this newfound autonomy came at a price. The Persian Empire, as a dominant force in the region, imposed its own conditions on the Greek city-states.

One of the key provisions of the Peace of Antalcidas was the requirement for all city-states to recognize the Persian king as the ultimate arbiter in disputes between Greek states. This gave the Persians significant control and influence over Greek affairs, effectively compromising the autonomy and sovereignty of the Greek city-states.

Additionally, the peace treaty stipulated that all Greek city-states should dismantle their walls and surrender any foreign possessions they held. This provision aimed to prevent any city-state from becoming too powerful or dominant, thereby maintaining a balance of power in the region that suited the interests of both Persia and Sparta.

The terms of the Peace of Antalcidas were met with mixed reactions among the Greek city-states. Some saw the treaty as a necessary step towards peace and stability after years of conflict, while others viewed it as a surrender to Persian influence and a betrayal of Greek autonomy.

The peace settlement had significant ramifications for Greek politics and society. The influence of Persia in Greece increased, as the Persian king played a role in mediating disputes and determining the fate of Greek city-states. This Persian intervention further complicated the political landscape of Greece and eroded the independence of the city-states.

The Peace of Antalcidas marked a shift in the balance of power in Greece. Sparta, which had emerged as the dominant force in the Peloponnesian War, used its alliance with Persia to solidify its position and exert influence over the Greek city-states. Athens, once a powerful empire, was relegated to a subordinate role in the new political order.

The peace settlement did not bring lasting stability to Greece. Discontent and tensions continued to simmer among the Greek city-states, leading to further conflicts and power struggles in the years that followed. The Peace of Antalcidas set the stage for the rise of new regional powers, such as Thebes and Macedon, which would eventually shape the course of Greek history.

The legacy of the Peace of Antalcidas is one of compromise, shifting alliances, and the enduring influence of external powers in Greek affairs. It serves as a reminder of the complexities of diplomacy and the challenges of maintaining autonomy in a world where powerful empires seek to assert their control.

As the Greek city-states navigated the aftermath of the Peloponnesian War and the terms of the peace settlement, they would continue to grapple with the ever-present question of balancing their own interests with the demands and pressures of external powers.

Chapter 17: Legacy of the Persian Wars

The victories of the Greek city-states over the Persian Empire in the Persian Wars left an indelible mark on Greek society and culture. The triumph of the Greeks against a powerful empire inspired a sense of national pride and a belief in the superiority of Greek civilization.

The Persian Wars became a significant theme in subsequent works of literature, art, and philosophy. Greek writers and historians, such as Herodotus and Thucydides, chronicled the events of the wars, emphasizing the bravery and resilience of the Greeks in the face of overwhelming odds. These accounts served not only as historical records but also as sources of inspiration for future generations.

The victories in the Persian Wars fueled a cultural flourishing in Greece known as the Golden Age. It was a time of intellectual and artistic achievement, where philosophers, playwrights, and artists thrived. The sense of national pride and the belief in Greek exceptionalism became embedded in the collective consciousness of the Greek city-states.

Greek philosophy, led by thinkers such as Socrates, Plato, and Aristotle, reached new heights during this period. These philosophers pondered questions of human nature, ethics, and the nature of reality. The legacy of the Persian Wars played a significant role in shaping their philosophical inquiries, as they sought to understand the nature of courage, justice, and the values that defined Greek society.

In the realm of art, the victories in the Persian Wars provided artists with a rich source of inspiration. Sculptures, paintings, and architectural works celebrated the heroes and battles of the wars, immortalizing their courage and sacrifice. The depiction of the Persian Wars in art served to reinforce the idea of Greek cultural superiority and the virtues of freedom and democracy.

Literature also flourished during this period. Playwrights like Aeschylus, Sophocles, and Euripides drew upon the Persian Wars as a backdrop for their tragedies, exploring themes of heroism, fate, and the consequences of war. These works not only entertained audiences but also served as a medium for reflecting on the human condition and the moral dilemmas faced by individuals and societies.

The legacy of the Persian Wars extended beyond the realms of culture and art. The victories instilled a belief in the power of democracy and individual freedom. The Greek city-states, particularly Athens, continued to champion democratic ideals and civic participation, shaping the political landscape for centuries to come.

Furthermore, the victories over the Persian Empire established a sense of Greek cultural and political identity. The concept of "Hellenism," which emphasized the shared language, customs, and values of the Greek city-states, emerged and served as a unifying force. Greek city-states, despite their internal conflicts, found common ground in their shared heritage and the memory of their triumphs over the Persians.

The legacy of the Persian Wars continued to reverberate throughout history. The stories and lessons learned from these conflicts influenced subsequent military strategies and campaigns. The Greek city-states' methods of warfare, including the use of phalanxes and naval tactics, had a lasting impact on military thinking and strategy in the Mediterranean region.

In summary, the victories of the Greek city-states over the Persian Empire in the Persian Wars had a profound and lasting impact on Greek society and culture. The wars became a significant theme in literature, art, and philosophy, fueling a cultural flourishing and inspiring a belief in Greek exceptionalism. The legacy of the Persian Wars shaped Greek identity, political ideals, and military strategies, leaving an enduring mark on the course of Western civilization.

Chapter 18: Alexander the Great

The memory of the Persian Wars, with its tales of Greek valor and resistance against the Persian Empire, continued to resonate in the Greek consciousness. It was against this backdrop that Alexander the Great, a student of the renowned philosopher Aristotle, embarked on his ambitious campaign to conquer the Persian Empire.

Born in 356 BCE, Alexander was the son of King Philip II of Macedon. Influenced by his tutor, Aristotle, Alexander was well-versed in the history and mythology surrounding the Persian Wars. He grew up with a deep sense of pride in his Greek heritage and a burning desire to avenge the past invasions of Greece by the Persians.

In 334 BCE, at the age of just 20, Alexander crossed the Hellespont with his army, beginning a military campaign that would eventually lead to the downfall of the mighty Persian Empire. His conquests were driven not only by a thirst for power and glory but also by a desire to exact revenge on the Persians for their previous aggressions.

As Alexander marched through Asia Minor, he encountered various Persian forces, many of whom were descendants of those who had fought against the Greeks in the Persian Wars. The memory of the past conflicts lingered, fueling Alexander's determination to prove the superiority of Greek arms and avenge the humiliations suffered by Greece.

In 331 BCE, at the Battle of Gaugamela, Alexander achieved a decisive victory over the Persian king, Darius III. This triumph not only solidified Alexander's control over the Persian Empire but also symbolized the fulfillment of the Greek quest for revenge against their ancient foes.

As Alexander continued his conquests, he sought to emulate the legendary Greek heroes who had fought against the Persians in the past. He revered figures like Achilles, who had displayed extraordinary courage and prowess in battle. Inspired by their example, Alexander led his troops from victory to victory, establishing a vast empire that stretched from Greece to Egypt and as far east as India.

In addition to his military successes, Alexander also sought to spread Greek culture and civilization to the conquered territories. He established cities modeled after Greek city-states, encouraged the adoption of Greek language and customs, and promoted the fusion of Greek and Persian cultures. This Hellenistic synthesis became a lasting legacy of Alexander's conquests.

The memory of the Persian Wars and the desire to avenge the past invasions played a significant role in shaping Alexander's actions and motivations. It fueled his determination to conquer the Persian Empire and assert Greek dominance in the region. Through his military achievements and the spread of Greek culture, Alexander the Great left an enduring impact on the course of history.

However, it is important to note that while Alexander's conquests were influenced by the memory of the Persian Wars, his campaign went beyond mere revenge. His vision extended far beyond the borders of Greece, and he aimed to create a vast empire that would unite diverse peoples under his rule. The memory of the Persian Wars served as a catalyst for his ambitions, but his ultimate goals and achievements surpassed the boundaries of a single conflict.

In conclusion, the memory of the Persian Wars played a significant role in the life and conquests of Alexander the Great. Inspired by the tales of Greek heroism and the desire to avenge past invasions, Alexander embarked on a military campaign that reshaped the world. His achievements left a lasting mark on history and further solidified the Greek legacy of triumph over the Persian Empire.

Chapter 19: Hellenistic Period

Following the death of Alexander the Great in 323 BCE, his vast empire fragmented into several Hellenistic kingdoms. This period, known as the Hellenistic era, witnessed the spread of Greek culture and the blending of Greek and local traditions across the conquered territories. The memory and influence of the Persian Wars played a significant role in shaping this transformative period in history.

The Hellenistic kingdoms that emerged, such as the Seleucid Empire, the Ptolemaic Kingdom, and the Antigonid Kingdom, adopted Greek administrative systems, language, and customs. Greek settlers, soldiers, and administrators migrated to these territories, bringing with them their cultural practices and ideas. The memory of the Persian Wars, with its tales of Greek valor and resistance, reinforced the Greeks' sense of cultural superiority and contributed to the spread of Greek culture throughout the Hellenistic world.

Greek art, architecture, literature, and philosophy flourished during the Hellenistic period. The influence of the Persian Wars can be seen in the themes and subject matter of these works. Artists depicted scenes from the Persian Wars and Greek victories against the Persians, emphasizing the heroism and bravery of Greek warriors. The memory of the past conflicts became intertwined with Hellenistic artistic expression, perpetuating the idea of Greek cultural superiority and the triumphs of the past.

In literature, writers like Callimachus, Theocritus, and Apollonius of Rhodes drew inspiration from the Persian Wars, incorporating elements of Greek mythology and historical events into their works. The memory of the Persian Wars served as a backdrop for epic poetry, tragic plays, and historical narratives, further reinforcing the cultural legacy of these conflicts.

The Hellenistic period also witnessed significant developments in philosophy. Philosophers like Epicurus, Zeno of Citium, and Pyrrho of Elis built upon the foundations laid by their predecessors, grappling with questions of ethics, metaphysics, and the nature of knowledge. The influence of the Persian Wars can be seen in their philosophical inquiries, as they sought to understand the complexities of human existence and the values that defined Greek society.

The spread of Greek culture during the Hellenistic period was not a one-sided process. Local traditions, customs, and artistic styles blended with Greek influences, giving rise to a rich and diverse cultural landscape. The encounter between Greek and Persian cultures, influenced by the memory of the Persian Wars, resulted in a fusion known as Greco-Persian syncretism. This syncretism is evident in the architecture, art, and religious practices of the Hellenistic period.

The legacy of the Persian Wars, with its tales of Greek heroism and resistance against the Persian Empire, played a significant role in shaping the Hellenistic period. It fueled a sense of Greek cultural superiority and inspired artistic and intellectual endeavors. The memory of the past conflicts became intertwined with Hellenistic identity and cultural expression, leaving a lasting impact on the development of the Hellenistic kingdoms.

In summary, the Hellenistic period witnessed the spread of Greek culture and the blending of Greek and local traditions across the conquered territories. The memory and influence of the Persian Wars played a crucial role in shaping this transformative era. Greek art, literature, philosophy, and cultural practices thrived, with the memory of the past conflicts serving as a source of inspiration and identity. The Hellenistic period stands as a testament to the enduring legacy of the Persian Wars and their impact on the development of Western civilization.

Chapter 20: Western Civilization

The Persian Wars stand as a crucial moment in the development of Western civilization, leaving an indelible mark on the course of history. The democratic ideals, cultural achievements, and military strategies of the Greeks during this period laid the foundation for future Western societies, shaping the trajectory of Western civilization.

The triumph of the Greek city-states against the mighty Persian Empire showcased the power of democracy and collective action. The Athenian model of democracy, which had emerged and matured during the years leading up to the Persian Wars, served as an inspiration for future democratic systems. The idea that citizens could actively participate in the governance of their society and have a voice in decision-making became a cornerstone of Western political thought.

Furthermore, the Persian Wars spurred a flourishing of Greek culture, art, and literature. The victories against the Persians instilled a sense of pride and confidence in the Greek city-states, leading to a period of cultural renaissance. The works of playwrights like Aeschylus, Sophocles, and Euripides, the philosophical inquiries of Socrates, Plato, and Aristotle, and the architectural marvels like the Parthenon in Athens all emerged during this time. These cultural achievements became touchstones of Western civilization, influencing subsequent generations and shaping the arts, sciences, and humanities for centuries to come.

The Persian Wars also left a lasting impact on military strategy and tactics. The innovative tactics employed by the Greeks, such as the use of hoplite infantry and the coordination of land and naval forces, became models for future military campaigns. The concept of a citizen-soldier, fighting for the ideals and freedom of their city-state, became ingrained in Western military traditions.

The legacy of the Persian Wars extended beyond the borders of ancient Greece. The stories of Greek heroism, resistance, and cultural achievement spread throughout the Mediterranean and beyond, influencing neighboring societies and civilizations. The encounters between Greek and Persian cultures, sparked by the wars, resulted in a vibrant exchange of ideas, technologies, and traditions.

The impact of the Persian Wars on Western civilization reverberates even in the present day. The concepts of democracy, individual freedoms, and civic engagement, which emerged during this time, continue to shape the political systems of Western societies. The cultural achievements and artistic masterpieces of ancient Greece continue to inspire and inform contemporary art, literature, and philosophy.

In conclusion, the Persian Wars were a pivotal moment in the development of Western civilization. The democratic ideals, cultural achievements, and military strategies of the Greeks during this period laid the groundwork for the future trajectory of Western societies. The memory of the Persian Wars serves as a reminder of the enduring legacy of ancient Greece and its profound influence on the shaping of Western civilization. It is a testament to the transformative power of human endeavors, the pursuit of freedom, and the enduring spirit of human creativity.

Don't miss out!

Visit the website below and you can sign up to receive emails whenever Christoffer Smestad publishes a new book. There's no charge and no obligation.

https://books2read.com/r/B-A-DDRW-ZYSJC

BOOKS2READ

Connecting independent readers to independent writers.

Also by Christoffer Smestad

Mind Matters: A Guide to Emotional Wellness
The Power of Manifestation: How to Bring Your Dreams to
Life
Addressing Climate Change and Human Health
AI in Action: A Comprehensive Guide to Real-world
Applications
The Ukraine-Russia Conflict
Resilience Unleashed: The Persian Wars' Impact
Warbound: Epic Tales of Troy

www.ingramcontent.com/pod-product-compliance
Lightning Source LLC
Chambersburg PA
CBHW022107150726
47990CB00003B/1267